*F*ollow us to
explore the
wonderful world
of young animals.

National Wildlife Federation

Library of Congress CIP Data: page 95.

RANGER RICK'S
WONDER
BOOK

HELLO, WORLD

Look out world, here come the newborn animals, full of life and ready to grow. On a prairie in Montana, this mother pronghorn (left) licks her newborn youngster clean, removing any smell that could attract a hungry coyote or other predator. In a cold mountain stream in Idaho, fish eggs that have been fertilized and buried in the gravel, slowly grow. One day they will be silvery, blue-green sockeye salmon. In a Georgia swamp, a mother alligator waits patiently as her green, scaly babies chip their way out of their buried eggs. Though these young animals don't really know it, a world of adventure lies ahead. Some animals, like most insects, fish, and snakes, are on their own from the time they are born. Other animals, like ducklings and even the pronghorn fawn, need the help of a parent. It takes years for elephants, apes, and people to become independent. They must learn how to find food, keep themselves clean, and avoid danger. The story of animals being born, growing up, and taking off on their own is full of excitement, danger, and wonder.

These blind, bald, and help-less newborn European dormice (1) have to wait two or three weeks before their eyes open and they can see the world around them. But only a month or so later they will be off and running, looking for food and finding homes of their own.

A baby zebra (2) looks ready to run even before it is free of its birth sac. In fact, a zebra can struggle to its feet only a few minutes after it is born. Less than half an hour later it will be strong enough to follow its mother to rejoin the herd.

The young kangaroo peeking from its mother's pouch (3) was smaller than a baby dormouse when it was born. It had to crawl through its mom's fur and into her pouch to nurse. The youngster, called a *joey*, stayed there for about six months before going outside. Even after it has stopped nurs-ing, the joey will hop back into the pouch for rest and safety until it is about ten months old.

7

Many kinds of baby birds look like they came into the world before they were completely ready. These pink, scrawny flickers (1) will have to wait at least ten days for their eyes to open. It will take another fifteen days or so for them to grow feathers and become strong enough to leave their nest.

This young wood duck (2) looks almost ready to run around even before it has pulled itself out of its shell. Wood ducks usually do jump out of the nest the day after they hatch and waddle along behind their mothers.

Baby bitterns (3) are more fully developed than young flickers, but less developed than ducks. Bitterns are born with their eyes open and with a light coat of down, but without any feathers. Their feathers grow in quickly, however, and they can fly away in about four weeks.

For turtles (1), snakes (2), and many other baby reptiles, it's *wham, bam,* off with their shells and out to see the world. There's no mom or dad around to help them. But for the American alligator (3), it's a different story. Even after laying her eggs and covering them with mud and sticks, the female alligator stays nearby to protect her nest. She's ready to chase away a nosy human or a hungry raccoon looking for eggs to eat. The young begin to hatch two months after the eggs have been laid. The mother chews open the nest to help her babies escape.

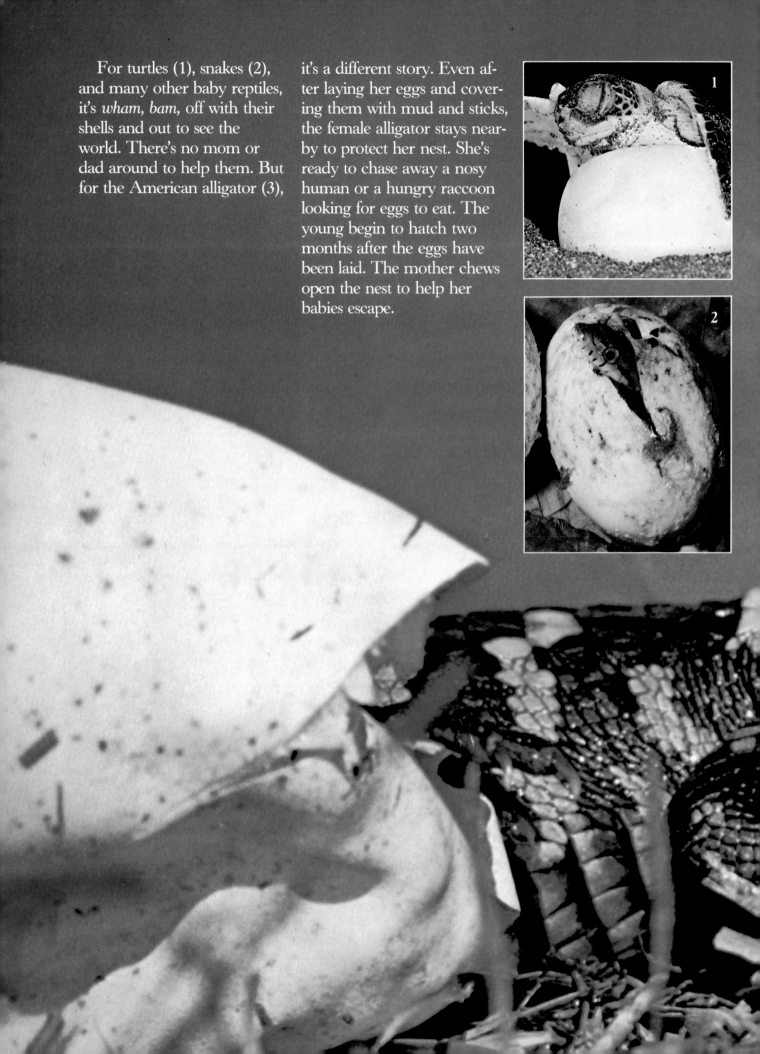

Frogs don't start out as frogs at all. Frogs' eggs (1) hatch under water and turn into long-tailed tadpoles, or pollywogs (2). They can be found in many ponds, streams, and swamps. Tadpoles wiggle through the water, munching on plants and tiny insects. As they become older, they slowly lose their tails and grow legs (3). They also lose the gills they needed for breathing under water and develop lungs for breathing on land. Some kinds of tadpoles take more than a year to

change into frogs. Others may
take only a few weeks. This
change is called *metamorphosis.*
When the change is complete,
the frog must poke its head
above the water to breathe (4).
It can also hop out onto the
land in search of insects to eat.

When I Grow Up...

Some young animals are easy to recognize. The newborn zebra shown on page 6 looks just like a zebra and no other animal. And there's little doubt that the animal shown hatching on pages 10 and 11 is an alligator. But many other animal youngsters look very different from their parents. It is hard to guess just which baby goes with which adult.

Look at the four pictures of young animals at the bottom of these two pages. Now look at the grownup animals just above them. Can you match the youngsters with the right adults? The answers are at the bottom of this page.

A. Opossum
B. Flamingo
C. Shrew
D. Crane

Answers:
C (2); D (3);
A (4); B (1);

15

LET'S EAT

Suppose newborn animals could talk. Their first words would be, "Let's eat!" Like this mouse in the corn, they are usually *hungry*. For many newborn animals, the first meal is no farther away than mom. Mammal mothers nurse their young on their own milk, which contains water, fats, vitamins, minerals, proteins, and sugar. The amount of each varies from animal to animal. Rhinos live in dry areas, and a mother rhino satisfies her babies' thirst by giving milk that includes a lot of water. Polar bear cubs live in the cold Arctic and need a lot of energy to grow quickly and stay warm. They get that energy from their mothers' milk, which is about one-third high-energy fat.

Many young birds get breakfast in bed, or at least in the nest. Keeping the chicks well-fed with insects, worms, and other food can be a full-time job for both mom and dad. A young kingfisher will eat twice its weight in food every day. If a newborn human ate as much for his size as a baby crow eats, in eight months he'd weigh about two hundred pounds. So anyone who says he eats like a bird either doesn't know birds—or is getting very, very fat!

Young robins (1) have such huge appetites that each parent must bring food to the nest every five to ten minutes. Pelican chicks (2) have to wait as their parents travel fifty miles or more in search of food. But two or three times a day the hungry youngsters have a feast as they dip deep into mom's or dad's pouch to help themselves to the food there. Cuckoo chicks don't get food from their parents at all. Mother cuckoos lay their eggs in the nests of other birds, who hatch the eggs. These other birds become substitute parents and feed the young cuckoos, even when the cuckoos become larger than they are (3)!

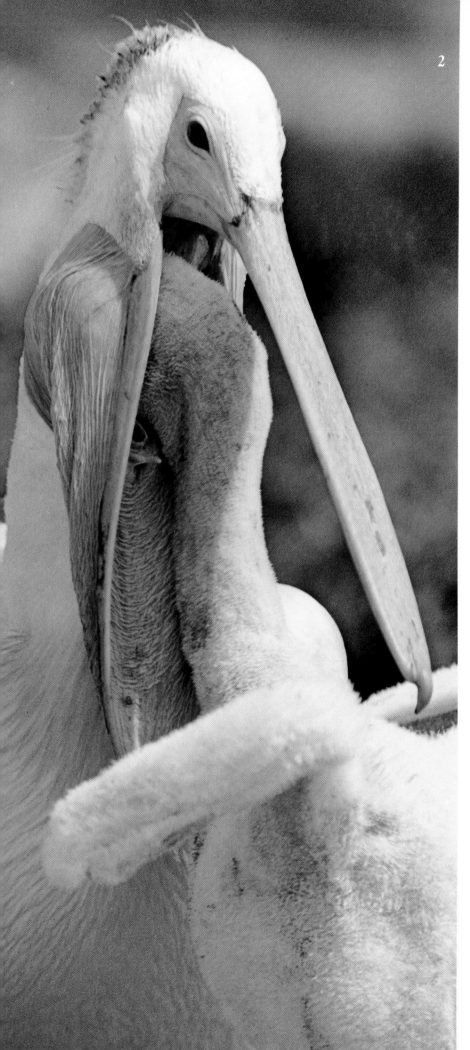

Newborn mammals usually feed on their mothers' milk until their first teeth appear. These young beavers are nursing now, but in two or three weeks they will be ready to eat leafy plants that their mother brings them. A month after that, they will stop drinking milk.

Young beavers, called *kits,* grow quickly. When they are six months old, their average weight is nearly sixteen pounds, about twenty times their weight at birth. By comparison, it takes a human baby six months just to double its weight.

Nothing beats a good, juicy worm. At least that's what this snake (1), salamander (2), and frog (3) seem to be saying. And for them, that's probably true. Earthworms provide the same amount of protein, ounce for ounce, as a good, juicy steak!

What's for Dinner?

The early bird gets the worm, but what does the early bat get? Or the early snake? Here are four predators, animals that eat other creatures. Which creatures do they eat? See if you can match the hunter with the animal that it likes for dinner. The answers are upside-down on the opposite page. Here's a small hint: predators don't always eat creatures smaller than themselves.

A

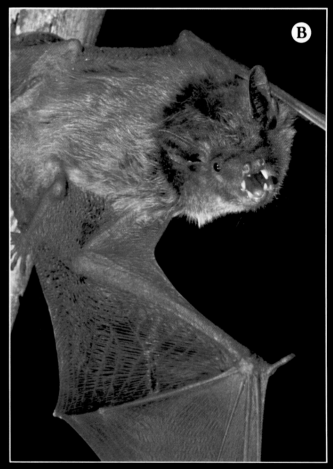

B

1

2

THE HUNTER

(A) King snake
(B) Bat
(C) Wolf
(D) Doodlebug

THE HUNTED

(1) Moth
(2) Moose
(3) Ant
(4) Copperhead

Answers:
(A) (4); (B) (1); (C) (2); (D) (3).

25

SNOOZING

After a big meal, cats love to curl up in a chair for a nap. And after a busy day, people think a cozy bed is a great place to be. But when do wild animals sleep? Do they take after-dinner naps? Do they snuggle into a soft nest for a full night's sleep?

Animals sleep, but not the way people do. Lions, like the male in the tree at left, can spend twenty hours a day resting and sleeping. Many animals doze off in short naps whenever they are drowsy. White rats may take as many as ten naps in twenty-four hours. Elephants take short naps, too, sleeping only about three to five hours a day. Baby elephants lie down, but most adult elephants sleep standing up.

Some animals, such as brown bats and woodchucks, sleep through the coldest part of the year. That kind of sleep is called hibernation. The animals' breathing and heartbeats slow down so the food their bodies have stored as fat lasts until warm weather.

It seems as if some animals can sleep almost anywhere. Airplane pilots have seen birds called swifts sleeping while flying two miles above the earth. In the ocean, seals and whales come to the surface for air without waking up.

Fish and snakes sleep with their eyes open because they don't have eyelids. How can they sleep with all that light around them? It's natural! After all, we can't close our ears, yet we sleep, sometimes through loud noises.

This yawning fox may be doing more than showing how tired it is. Yawning takes in extra oxygen to be used by the brain and tired muscles, but it can also send messages to other animals. An animal may yawn to warn or scare away an enemy, attract a mate, or tell members of its group that it's time to stop playing or fighting.

Birds sleeping while standing on one leg may look uncomfortable, but they aren't. These flamingos are actually resting the muscles in their drawn-up legs. If something frightens the birds, they can bring their raised legs down quickly for a running takeoff.

The European dormouse (1) is a *very* sleepy fellow. In fact, part of its name comes from the Latin word *dormire,* meaning "to sleep." It spends half the year (from October to April) in hibernation, occasionally waking up to eat a quick snack of hazelnuts and then falling back asleep. When hibernating, the dormouse sleeps so soundly you could roll it around without waking it up!

Young rabbits like these baby cottontails (2) do not hibernate during the winter as the dormice do. They also don't sleep very long at any one time. Instead, they take up to twenty short naps a day. No wonder the tortoise was able to win that race with the hare!

The hedgehog (3) hunts for food during the night and spends its days sleeping somewhere in a nest of dead leaves. The hedgehog's prickly spines protect it from being eaten by another animal while it sleeps.

ONE OF THE GANG

C all it a herd, a clan, or a school. Whatever word you use, "it" is still the same thing: a group of animals living together. Can you imagine growing up in a family with dozens or even hundreds of grownups and youngsters? For some animals, that is the only way of life they know—whether it's a flock of fifty ostriches, a clan of eight chimps, a herd of a dozen giraffes, or a colony of a million penguins (left).

What are the advantages of growing up in such large groups? The animals are often safer than when they grow up alone. Musk oxen and baboons are good examples. When wolves threaten the oxen or lions attack young baboons, the adults move close together. This way they make a living wall between their youngsters and the enemies trying to attack them.

Finding food can be easier when a large group looks for it. But what happens to the youngsters while the grownups hunt? In swarms of bees and packs of wolves, some of the adults stay at home as babysitters while other adults go out searching for food.

When fur seals are born,
they find themselves in a crowd
of thousands of other fur seals.
Dozens of pups have the same
father because a single mature
male keeps as many as forty
females in his territory. While
their mothers are away searching for food in the sea, the
pups form groups of their own
called "pup pods."

Young elephants grow up in a herd that is actually a big family. The herd often includes a grandma elephant and several "aunts" that all help take care of the young ones. The older males usually live by themselves away from the herd. Really big herds—those that have fifty or more animals—may include the members of many different elephant families.

As the elephants roam about looking for food, they purr, almost like cats. But if one of them spots danger, it stops purring. The silence warns the others that something is wrong.

A School of Fish

Sometimes groups of animals are known by special names. Most of us know that a group of fish is called a *school*. But, did you know that a group of foxes is called a *skulk*, a group of toads is called a *knot*, or that a group of goldfinches is called a *charm*?

See how many of the mammals and birds listed here you can match correctly with their group names:

Answers:
MAMMALS
1. (c); 2. (e); 3. (a); 4. (b); 5. (d).
BIRDS
1. (e); 2. (a); 3. (d); 4. (b); 5. (c).

MAMMALS

1. A leap of _____ (a) elephants
2. A pride of _____ (b) rabbits
3. A herd of _____ (c) leopards
4. A hutch of _____ (d) kangaroos
5. A troop of _____ (e) lions

BIRDS

1. A gaggle of _____ (a) quail
2. A covey of _____ (b) chickens
3. A paddling of __ (c) turkeys
4. A peep of _____ (d) ducks
5. A rafter of _____ (e) geese

PIGGY-BACKING

A cross the river and through the trees, some animal youngsters ride piggy-back on mom as she takes off swimming, swinging, or climbing. Riding piggyback is a game or a special treat for people. For the animals, it is an important part of growing up. The youngsters need to stay near their mothers if they are to survive. By hanging on tightly, they can be with their mothers as they move about searching for food or escaping enemies. At the same time, the mothers can move farther and faster if they don't have to wait for junior tagging along behind.

Young baboons start out holding tightly to mom's chest so they can nurse and ride at the same time. As they grow bigger, they switch sides and travel on their mom's back. It's not unusual to see a mother koala heading up a gum tree while carrying a youngster that's half as big as she is (left). But the chimp and the opossum have even bigger problems. Mother chimp may have an older offspring on her back while her newest baby is hanging on in front, nursing. Mother opossum has to carry around a half dozen or so youngsters, even after they have grown to nearly half her size.

Swimming can be dangerous for baby grebes (1) and hippo calves (2). Large fish may gobble up the young birds, and crocodiles sometimes snatch stray hippo calves. For these youngsters, few places seem as safe as mom's back.

Climbing trees can be dangerous too—especially for the youngster hanging on. But the Australian ring-tailed possum (3) has something that makes the job a lot easier and safer: a long, grasping tail. Mom uses hers for holding onto branches, and junior uses his to hold onto mom.

Bats, frogs, spiders, and scorpions may seem creepy to some folks. But to young bats, frogs, spiders, and scorpions, there's no place like mom—or dad. A mother vampire bat (1) can even fly with her youngster hanging on tightly with its tiny claws. This female holding her baby is resting. The male in front of her looks like he's ready to attack the person who took the picture.

When two hundred or so spiderlings hitch a ride on mom wolf spider's back (2), they have to hold on tightly. If one falls off, mom leaves it behind.

Tadpoles of the arrow-poison frog ride on their father's back (3) where they grow bigger and stronger. Eventually the frog

dunks the tadpoles in water and they swim away.

Scorpion babies can ride safely on their mom's back and even right next to her poison-filled stinger (4). The real danger comes when the youngsters drop off. They must be careful so mom doesn't mistake one of them for prey and eat it for her dinner.

This tiny alligator riding
on its mom's snout shows an
unusual case of motherly care
in the reptile world. Most
baby reptiles never see their
mothers, who lay the eggs
and then leave them. But
not young alligators. Their
mothers do their best to protect their youngsters. In fact,
newborn alligators sometimes
ride safely *inside* mom's
mouth as she takes her young
from the nest to the water.

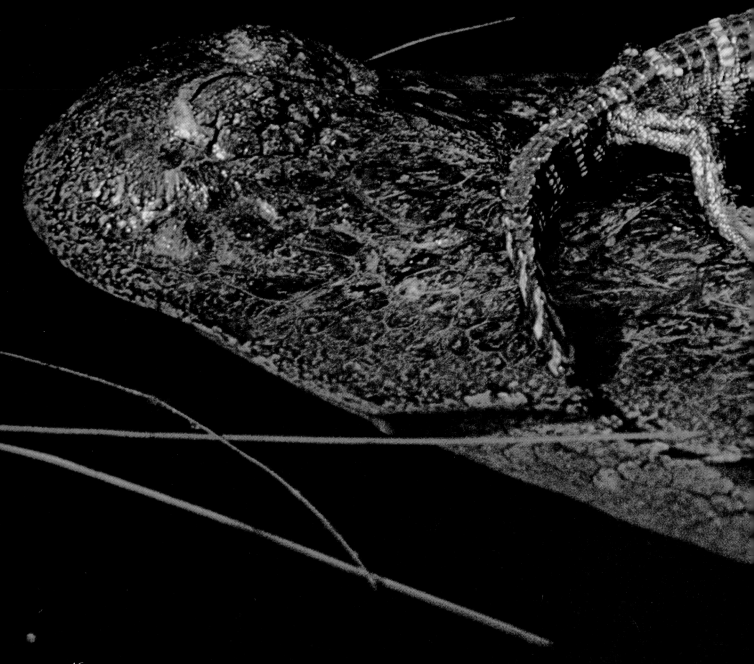

LET'S EXPLORE

Young animals spend a lot of time exploring. That is how they get the knowledge and develop the instincts they need to survive. By exploring, the animals find new places to live, hunt, and hide. A field mouse being chased by an owl is in real danger of being killed. If the mouse has explored the nearby brush and holes, it will know where to run to safety.

Some animals, like the raccoon at left, are natural explorers. They are born with an urge to wander off on their own. By the time they are old enough to be independent, they just walk away from home on one more trip and don't return. Other young animals must be forced by their parents to go into new places or to try new activities. Otters spend much of their adult lives in water, but sometimes young otters are afraid to dive in for the first time. Then it's up to mom to shove them in!

Though many animals learn important lessons by exploring, some animals seem to explore just for the fun of it. Chimpanzees in captivity will do chores for the reward of getting to play with new objects.

What makes animals explore and take chances? Some scientists believe the animals are simply curious. There is an old saying that curiosity killed the cat. The truth is, curiosity has helped cats and other creatures learn more about their world and how to survive in it.

On their first trips away from home, baby mountain lions (1) find that a small fallen tree is a real challenge to climb over. As they grow, the cubs learn to sneak through the forest at night in search of deer, elk, and even birds.

With almost no feathers, this young cattle egret clinging to a limb (2) isn't going to get very far away from its nest. Newborn egrets must wait about six weeks before they can fly. In the meantime, they get ready by flapping their wings to exercise their flight muscles. Sometimes the young birds fall out of their nest. If they can't climb back in, they may starve or get eaten by hungry predators.

A black bear cub has no problem climbing a tree (3). It could climb trees before it could walk very well! On the ground, curious and nose to nose with a bumblebee (4), the cub can rely on its thick fur to keep from being stung. Later it will even eat honeybees as it pulls the honey from their hives in hollow trees.

These opossums were carried in their mother's pouch for two months before they emerged to explore the world. Now, using their large, sensitive eyes, they wander through the darkness in search of the insects, frogs, and other small animals they like to eat. At the same time, they need to watch out for their enemies, especially foxes, bobcats, hawks, and owls. Opossums are slow and clumsy on the ground. That is why they usually climb trees when they are scared or threatened. If they can't reach safety, they sometimes just lie still and play dead.

LET'S PLAY

You're it! Games like tag, follow-the-leader, and king-of-the-hill are great fun to play with friends on summer days. Many young animals also play games. Mountain goats butt heads in mock battles, kangaroos box, bear cubs and baby tigers wrestle, and foxes and wolves play tag.

Young animals look like they are having fun playing, and they are learning valuable lessons that may save their lives. By playing, they improve their ability to hunt food and defend themselves.

Kittens and cubs strengthen muscles and sharpen hunting skills by chasing, wrestling, stalking, crouching, and springing. When animals like gorillas and badgers play with other members of their groups, they increase their sense of belonging to a close family.

Playing also helps some animals become more important than other members of their groups. Among baboons, lions, and seals, for example, the animals that are the strongest and the quickest when playing usually lead their former playmates when they grow up.

Animals need to play to grow up normally. Monkeys that are raised alone and don't get to play with other monkeys usually become very shy or vicious. Many of them cannot successfully attract mates later in life because they never learned how to get along with others of their kind. Playing helps animals stay healthy and learn how to live in a world where survival is the name of the game!

When young foxes play, it looks like a battle! They chase each other, wrestle, and pretend to fight. Though they growl and bite, they usually don't hurt each other. If the play-fighting gets too rough and a pup wants to stop, it rolls over on its back and wags its tail. This signal tells the others, "You win. I give up."

Dolphins are among the most intelligent and playful animals in the sea. They chase each other, push or balance floating objects with their flippers or noses, and seem to enjoy leaping up to thirty-five feet into the air! Dolphins even like to surf. They have been seen riding big waves into shore, just as people on surf boards do. Dolphins sometimes follow ships just to ride the waves the ships make! When dolphins do this, they can reach speeds of thirty to thirty-five miles per hour.

Dueling with their tusks helps elephants (1) learn how strong they are and which animals in the herd they can boss around. These friendly battles also teach the elephants how to defend themselves.

Young prairie dogs (2) play tag and wrestle with their neighbors. These games strengthen group ties and help keep the prairie dog town one big, happy family.

Young Siberian tigers (3) look like big playful kittens. They chase each other, wrestle, and swat one another with their paws. Their rough-and-tumble games help them develop the stalking and hunting skills they will need when they get older.

After a long day of fishing and playing, it sure feels good to rest by a cool stream and take in the sights!

As young mammals grow older, they play less often. One day they will be old enough to take care of themselves. Then most of their time will be spent hunting, finding mates, having their own families, and watching their offspring play games and grow up.

HIDE AND SEEK

eady or not, here I come! There's nothing more fun than a game of hide and seek, at least for human children. But for animals, hide and seek is not a game. To survive, some predators and prey must blend into their surroundings and disappear. This ability to hide in plain sight is one of Nature's best tricks. It is called "camouflage."

The stripes on the coats of the tiger cubs at left blend in with the shadows and shapes of plants in the forest. That helps them remain unseen as they creep up close to surprise their prey.

Polar bears and snowy owls are white like the arctic snow around them and that lets them hunt without being seen. Brightly colored tropical fish easily hide among the colored corals of their reef homes. The colors and patterns on the backs of some snakes help them to hide in grass or leaves, and many times frogs can't be seen by enemies because they are as green as the ponds in which they live.

Some animals change color when the seasons change. In the summer, ptarmigans and snowshoe rabbits are brown; but as winter arrives, they turn white. Their white coats help them hide in the snow. Other animals, like shrimp, octopuses, and chameleons, can change colors quickly to match the color of their surroundings. One minute an octopus might be brown. The next minute it might be red or blue! And you thought *you* were good at playing hide and seek!

Young animals don't always do the right thing when danger threatens. Most of them try to hide when they are scared. Sometimes, though, they get confused and don't know where to go! When this happens, the ways they try to hide can be very funny.

The bear cub (1) chose the *right* place to hide—behind its

mom. Mother bear is sure to protect it from enemies.

This baby western sea gull (2) chose the *wrong* spot to hide. A cool, dark place under a rock would be a great place to escape from the hot sun or from enemies, but this inexperienced little chick is trying to get into a spot that is much too small for it!

This young orangutan in a mud puddle (3) seems to be trying to hide, but it probably isn't. When an orangutan really wants to get away from danger, it usually climbs a tree. So, all this youngster is doing is having fun splashing itself with water.

Is it the Creature from the Green Lagoon? No, it's just a young gallinule (4) covered with green duckweed. If this bird is trying to hide, then it's not doing too well. We can see the bird, but it can't see us because the duckweed is over its eyes.

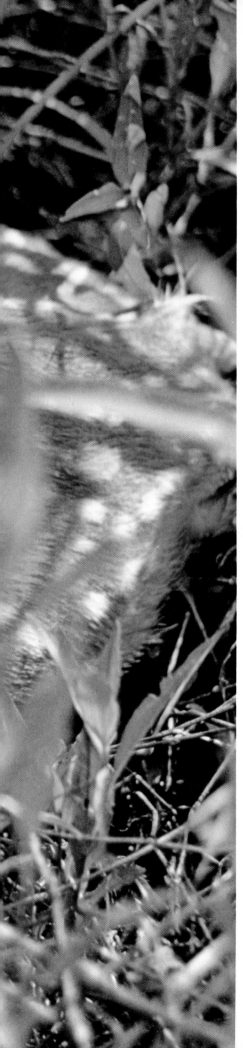

A newborn fawn can't run away from danger very fast, but its spotted coat and lack of odor help keep it hidden from enemies. The spots on a fawn's coat blend in so well with the patches of sun and shadow in the grass that a hungry predator may pass right by a motionless fawn and never see it.

The black, brown, and tan feathers of these baby wood-cocks match the colors of the dead leaves on the ground. Predators, such as foxes, won't notice the birds unless they move or make a noise.

Find the Hidden Animals

Ranger Rick is looking for some of his friends, but their camouflage is so good he can't see them. Can you help him find the moth, the frog, the flounder, and the sargassum fish in the pictures below?

ANSWERS:

A. Flounder
B. Moth
C. Frog
D. Sargassum
   Fish

71

SNUGGLING AND NUZZLING

Snow monkey mothers, like the one at left, snuggle their babies by rocking and cradling them gently in their arms. Fox, mountain lion, and bear youngsters pile over each other and huddle close to their mothers. In fact, many kinds of animals do like to cuddle together, holding and touching each other softly. They do this for several reasons.

Some mammals, such as mice and hamsters, are born without any hair. They need their mother's body heat to stay warm until their hair grows in. If some of these animals get too cold, they just stop growing until they warm up.

When an adult male rabbit nuzzles, or rubs noses, with baby rabbits, the babies pick up a special odor from glands on his chin. That odor marks them all as members of the same group and helps keep them from fighting each other. Some animal mothers, like giraffes and fur seals, nuzzle their babies to learn what they smell like. That's really helpful for mothers who join other parents and rear their young in groups. Often these mothers must leave the group to search for food. When they return, they can pick out their own offspring from the others in the crowd by the youngsters' special smells and cries.

When a family of mountain lions (1) snuggles together, it's time for fun. If a strange kitten were to join them, the youngsters would fight it. That's not very likely to happen, though, since mountain lions live far apart in the wild.

Emperor penguins (2) are hatched by their fathers. First, the father balances the egg on top of his feet and covers it with a fold of skin to keep it warm. Once hatched, the chicks grow quickly and go off to snuggle with other youngsters as the adults search for food in the sea.

As a Dall sheep (3) nuzzles its mother's face, it licks off and swallows bacteria it needs to digest the grass it eats. The

youngster will also nuzzle mature males as a way of paying respect to the adults.

Rock hyraxes (4) spread out all over each other as they warm themselves in the sun. By facing in several directions, they can see enemies—such as eagles, pythons, and leopards —no matter which direction they come from.

75

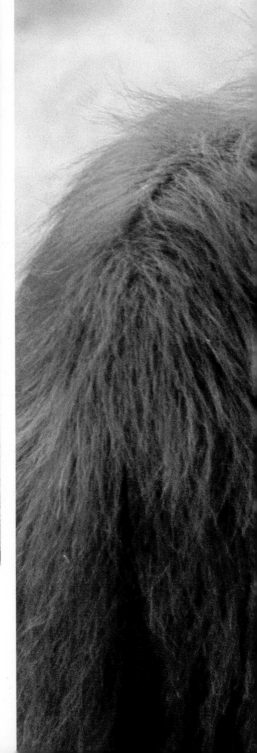

Mother seals and their pups (1) often rub noses. When the mother nuzzles her baby, she breathes in the youngster's smell and remembers it. She depends on this scent to help her pick out her own pup when it is lost in a crowd of other seals.

With a nudge and a lick, a mother moose can calm down her scared calf (2), letting it know that everything is all right. She also nudges the calf to make it stay by her side in case there really is some danger nearby, perhaps a hungry wolf on the prowl.

A young orangutan snuggles cozily in its mother's arms (3) for several months before it learns to walk, going with her wherever she goes. Sucking on its mother's finger probably makes this wide-eyed youngster feel safe. Later it will play with other young orangutans, but it will still come back to mom for security.

3

LICK, SPLASH, AND SCRATCH

Keeping clean is important when you live outdoors and have only one set of feathers, fur, or scales to wear. Licking, grooming, scratching, and preening take up much of an animal's time. These activities help keep animals free from mites, fleas, and other harmful parasites. For animals, keeping clean is keeping healthy!

When deer, cats, squirrels, and other mammals have babies, the first thing they do is lick them clean and dry them. Mothers, like the lioness at left, continue to clean their young until they are able to clean themselves. Licking also helps the mother identify her young. If baby goats are taken away at birth and cleaned before the mother licks them, she will act as if they are strangers when they are returned to her.

Animals sometimes get an itch where they can't scratch or lick. When this happens, animals such as monkeys and prairie dogs run their fingers through each other's fur and remove dirt and insects. This is called *grooming*. The animal being groomed gets its itch scratched, and the groomer is rewarded with a tasty bug and maybe salt and vitamin D from the other animal's skin and fur. Animals such as bears, elephants, and bison rub against nearby trees and rocks or roll around on the ground. They'll do almost anything to relieve that awful itch!

Like most birds, this roseate spoonbill (1) loves to splash in water. Bathing helps keep a bird's feathers clean, and it is part of a process that keeps birds from getting cold.

After bathing, birds, like this mallard (2), use their beaks to nibble and peck each feather from bottom to top. This is called *preening*. By preening, a bird removes parasites and dirt and takes oil from a gland near its tail and spreads it all over its feathers. This oil water-proofs the feathers to keep the bird warm and dry. When a bird preens it also straightens feathers that are out of place so it can fly more easily.

Elephants (3) enjoy baths, in water . . . and in dust! They use their trunks to shower themselves with water, and then sometimes throw dust over their backs. The water cools them off, and the dust protects them from insect bites and the hot sun.

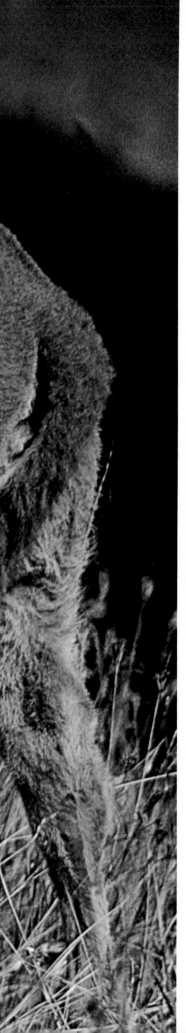

When the weather starts to get warm, animals like this bison and walrus itch more and more. That is because fleas, ticks, flies, and other biting insects are most active in the summer. For many animals, there is no escape until the frosts come in the fall and kill the pests. Until then, it's lick, splash, and scratch for relief.

LEARNING TO SURVIVE

Before young animals are ready to be independent, they must know how to find and capture their own food.

Plant eaters have no real problem. They may need to learn which plants to eat and which to leave alone, but once food is found, they simply eat until they are full.

For meat eaters, life isn't that simple. They must catch prey that is trying very hard not to get caught and eaten. Some creatures, including snakes, spiders, and lizards, are born knowing how to hunt. They may need a bit of practice before they are very good, but they don't need anyone to show them how to do it.

Other animals must be taught. Lion cubs need about a year to grow strong enough and learn enough skills to hunt for themselves. Brown bear cubs like those at left may also be a year old before they are ready to leave home. The lions and the bears learn by watching their parents or other adults.

Some birds also have to take hunting—or fishing—lessons. Young frigate birds, which live on tropical islands, spend hours each day practicing the methods their parents have perfected. By the time the youngsters have become adults, they will have learned how to scoop up flying fish skimming just above the surface of the ocean. They will also have learned how to attack other sea birds and force them to give up whatever fish they have caught. The frigate birds then catch the lost meal before it hits the water.

To capture prey, hunters do a lot of chasing, poking, and splashing. The bobcat (1) hot on the trail of a deermouse must time its leap just right. Jumping too soon or too late could mean another lost lunch.

If this young mountain lion (2) is looking for an easy meal, it's going to be disappointed. The desert tortoise, though slow, is protected by its shell from the hungry kitten.

A young raccoon (3) splashing in the water uses a keen sense of touch to find tasty crayfish, tadpoles, minnows, and frogs. This splashing in shallow water led some people to think, mistakenly, that raccoons wash their food.

3

Like lion and bear cubs, cheetah cubs learn how to hunt by watching, following, and imitating their mother. First, they practice sneaking quietly through the grass without being seen or smelled by their prey. By the time they are seven months old, the cubs are ready for a real hunt. They are still too small to catch any-thing, so mom helps them. She catches an animal herself and then lets it go for the cubs to chase and attack.

At sixteen months, the cubs are fully grown and out on their own. Adult cheetahs are the fastest four-legged animals on earth. Even the swift gazelle is no match for their 65-mile-per-hour sprints.

Nature's successful hunters have developed many ways to capture prey. The snowy owl (1) of the Arctic perches silently for hours before it swoops down to grab a lemming or a hare. The owl in the photo has snagged an eider, a duck that grows as large as the owl itself.

The chameleon (2) uses its long, sticky tongue to snap up

this dragonfly or spiders and butterflies. The chameleon's strong tail lets it grip branches tightly as it reaches out farther and farther for its prey. Even if its tail were to slip, the chameleon could survive a fall of forty feet or more.

The Asian archerfish (3) is an expert target shooter that spits out droplets of water at bugs on branches. When an insect is knocked into the water, the fish gulps it down. An adult archerfish can hit small prey three feet away.

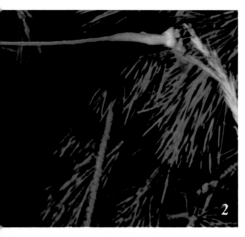

Getting Away...

Animals must do more than find food if they are to survive. They must also avoid being eaten by other creatures. Many animals run away when threatened, but there are other ways to get away from danger.

A skunk (1) chases off its enemies with a strong spray of bad-smelling fluid. A hedgehog (2) curls up into a ball, leaving its sharp spines sticking out to prick any animal that tries to attack it. The hog-nosed snake (3)

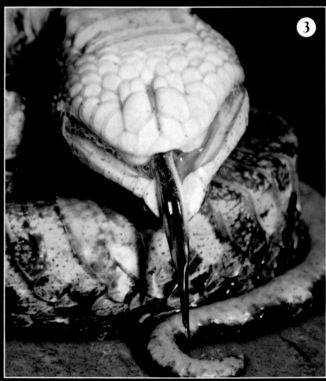

Answers:
A. c; B. a; C. d, D. b.

simply rolls over and plays dead. Since some predators only attack moving animals, they will often leave this "dead" snake alone. The hawk moth (4) scares its enemies away by spreading its wings to reveal bright spots that look like huge eyes.

Here are some more animals that have unusual ways of getting out of trouble. Can you tell which animal does what? The answers are at the bottom of the opposite page.

A. The _____ rolls into a ball, protected by its hard shell.

B. Like the hog-nosed snake, the _____ also rolls over and plays dead.

C. The _____ breaks off part of its tail when caught and runs away to safety.

D. The _____ gives off a bad-smelling liquid that drives the enemy away.

   a. Opossum   c. Armadillo

   b. Grasshopper   d. Lizard

INDEX

Illustrations are in **bold face** type.

Alligator: 5, 10, **10-11,** 14, 46, **46-47**
Ant: 25, **25**
Ant Lion (Doodlebug): 25, **25**
Archerfish: 91, **91**
Armadillo: 93

Baboon: 33, 41, 55
Badger: 55
Bat: 24, **24,** 25, 27
   vampire, 44, **44**
Bear: 55, 73, 79, 88
   Alaskan brown, **62-63, 84,** 85
   black, 50, **51**
   grizzly, 66, **66,** 67
   polar, 17, 65
Beaver: 20, **20-21**
Bee: 33
   bumblebee, 50, **51**
   honeybee, 50
Birth: 4-12
   hatching, 5, **8,** 9, **9,** 10, **10-11,** 12, **12,** 74
Bison: 79, **82-83,** 83
Bobcat: 52, 86, **86**

Camouflage: **64,** 65, **68-69,** 69, 70, **70-71**
Cat: 27, 37, 49, 79
Chameleon: 65, 90-91, **90-91**
Cheetah: 88, **88-89**
Chicken: 39
Chimpanzee: 33, 41, 49
Cleaning: 78-83
   bathing, 80, **80-81**
   grooming, 79
   licking, **78,** 79
   preening, 79, 80, **80**
   scratching, 79, **82-83,** 83
Climbing: **40, 42,** 43, **48,** 50, **50-51,** 52, **52-53**
Crane: 15, **15**
Crow: 17
Cuckoo: 18, **19**

Dall Sheep: 74, **75**
Deer: 50, **68-69,** 69, 79
Defense: 55, 65, 92-93, **92-93**
Dolphin: **58-59,** 59

Dragonfly: 91, **91**
Duck: 5, **38,** 39, 80, **80**
   eider, 90, **90**
   wood, 9, **9**

Eating: 16-25, 84-92
Egret: 50, **51**
Elephant: 5, 27, 37, **36-37,** 39, 60, **60-61,** 79, 80, **81**
Exploring: 48-53

Fighting: 73, 74
Fish: 27, 38, **38,** 65
   flounder, 70, 71, **71**
   flying, 85
   raccoon butterflyfish, **39**
   sargassum, 70, 71, **71**
Flamingo: **14,** 15, 28, **28-29**
Flicker: 9, **9**
Flying: 9, 44, 50, 85
Fox: 28, **28,** 38, 52, 55, 56, **56, 57,** 69, 73
Frigate Bird: 85
Frog: 12, 13, **13,** 22, **22-23,** 52, 65, 86
   arrow poison, 44, **45**
   camouflaged, 70, **70,** 71
   tadpole, 12, **12,** 13, 86

Gallinule: 67, **67**
Gazelle: 88, **89**
Giraffe: 33, 73
Goat: 79
Goldfinch: 38
Goose: 39
Gorilla: 55
Grasshopper: 93
Grebe: **42,** 43
Group Behavior: 32-39, 55

Hamster: 73
Hedgehog: 30, **31,** 92, **92**
Hibernation: 27, 30
Hiding: 64-71
Hippopotamus: **2-3, 42-43,** 43, **54**
Hunting: 33, 34, 37, 55, 60, 63, 84-91
Hyrax: 75, **75**

Kangaroo: **6-7,** 7, **38,** 39, 55

Kingfisher: 17
Koala: **40,** 41

Least Bittern: **8,** 9
Leopard: 39, 75
Lion: **26,** 27, 33, 39, 55, **78,** 79, 85, 88
Lizard: 85, 93

Metamorphosis: 12-13, **12-13**
Monkey: 55, 79
   snow, **72,** 73
Moose: 24, 25, **76,** 77
Moth: 24, 25, 70, **70,** 71
   hawk, 93, **93**
Mountain Goat: 55
Mountain Lion: 50, **50,** 73, 74, **74,** 86, **86**
Mouse: 73
   deermouse, **16,** 17, 86, **86**
   dormouse, **6,** 7, 30, **30**
   field, 49
Musk Ox: 33

Nursing: 7, 17, 20, **20-21**
Nuzzling: 72-77

Octopus: 65
Opossum: **14,** 15, **15,** 41, 52, **52-53,** 93
Orangutan: **66,** 67, **76-77,** 77
Otter: 49
Owl: 49, 52
   snowy, 65, 90, **90-91**

Pelican: 18, **18-19**
Penguin: **32,** 33, 74, **74-75**
Piggybacking: 40-47
Playing: 54-63
Prairie Dog: 60, **60,** 79
Pronghorn: **4,** 5
Ptarmigan: 65

Quail: 39

Rabbit: 30, **30-31,** 39, 65, 73
Raccoon: 10, **48,** 49, 86, **87**
Rat: 27, 49
Rhinoceros: 17
Ring-tailed Possum: **42,** 43

Kingfisher: 17
Robin: 18, **18**
Roseate Spoonbill: 80, **80**

Salamander: 22, **22**
Scent: 5, 69, 73, 77, 88, 92
Scorpion: 44, **45**
Sea Gull: **66,** 67
Seal: 27, 34, **34-35,** 55, 73, **76,** 77
Shrew: 14, 15, **15**
Shrimp: 65
Skunk: 92, **92**
Sleeping: 26-31, **26, 28-29, 30-31**
Snake: 24, 27, 65, 85, 93
   copperhead, 25, **25**
   garter, 22, **22**
   hog-nosed, 92, **92,** 93
   king, **24,** 25
   python, 75
   rat, 10, **10**
Snuggling: 72-77
Sockeye Salmon: 5
Spider: 85, 91
   wolf, 44, **44-45**
Squirrel: 79
Swift: 27
Swimming: **12-13, 42-43,** 43, 44, 49, 59

Tiger: 55, 60, **61, 64,** 65
Toad: 38
Tortoise: 30, 86, **86**
Turkey: 39
Turtle: 10, **10**

Walrus: 83, **83**
Whale: 27
Wolf: 25, **25,** 33, 55, 77
Woodchuck: 27
Woodcock: 69, **69**
Worm: 17, 22, **22, 23,** 24

Zebra: **6,** 7, 14

ILLUSTRATION CREDITS

All Ranger Rick art in this book is by Alton Langford.

Cover: John Shaw. Pages 2-3: F. S. Mitchell/Tom Stack & Associates.

HELLO WORLD

Page 4: Frank R. Martin. 6: (top) Norman Myers/Bruce Coleman, Inc.; (bottom) Hans Reinhard/Bruce Coleman, Inc. 6-7: Hans and Judy Beste. 8: Siebe Rekker. 9: (top) Dwight R. Kuhn; (bottom) Dr. William Weber. 10: (top) David Hughes/Bruce Coleman, Inc.; (middle) Animals Animals/Zig Leszczynski. 10-11: Wendell D. Metzen. 12: (top) Jane Burton/Bruce Coleman, Inc.; (middle) Dr. E. R. Degginger; (bottom) Andrew Skolnick. 13: Herman Eisenbeiss/National Audubon Society Collection/Photo Researchers. 14: (top left) Sam Blakesley/Photri; (bottom left) M. P. Kahl; (top right) Robert L. Dunne; (bottom right) Dwight R. Kuhn. 15: (top left) Rod Planck; (bottom left) Joseph Van Wormer; (top right) George W. Archibald; (bottom right) Jack Dermid.

LET'S EAT

Page 16: Bruce Thomas. 18: Jack Dermid. 18-19: Lynn M. Stone. 19: John Markham/Bruce Coleman, Inc. 20-21: Wolfgang Bayer. 22: (top) John MacGregor; (bottom) Lynn M. Stone. 22-23: Dwight R. Kuhn. 24: (top left) Jack Dermid; (bottom left) Stephen Dalton/NHPA;

(top right) Laura Riley; (bottom right) G. C. Kelley. 25: (top left) Robert L. Dunne; (bottom left) Raymond A. Mendez/Animals Animals; (top right) Robert Mitchell/Animals Animals; (bottom right) Joe McDonald.

SNOOZING

Page 26: Martin W. Grosnick. 28: Tom Walker. 28-29: M. Austerman/Animals Animals. 30: Jane Burton/National Audubon Society Collection/Photo Researchers. 30-31: Gene C. Frazier. 31: Jane Burton/Bruce Coleman, Inc.

ONE OF THE GANG

Page 32: Bruno J. Zehnder. 34-35: Stephen J. Krasemann/DRK Photo. 36-37: Sven Lindblad/National Audubon Society Collection/Photo Researchers. 38: (top) Don Cornelius; (middle) Erwin and Peggy Bauer; (lower left) Fred and Dixie Burnett. 39: Ed Robinson/Tom Stack & Associates.

PIGGYBACKING

Page 40: Jean-Paul Ferrero/Ardea. 42: (top center) Charles G. Summers, Jr.; (middle left) Michael Morcombe. 42-43: Charles G. Summers, Jr. 44: Nina Leen, LIFE Magazine © 1966 Time Inc. 44-45: Robert W. Mitchell. 45: (top) Dr. Edward S. Ross; (bottom) Robert W. Mitchell. 46-47: Thase Daniel.

LET'S EXPLORE

Page 48: Gary Meszaros. 50: Zig Leszczynski/Animals Animals. 51:

(bottom left) Charles H. Meitzen; (top) Jack Couffer/Bruce Coleman, Inc.; (bottom right) G. C. Kelley. 52-53: Leonard Maynard.

LET'S PLAY

Page 54: Tom McHugh/National Audubon Society Collection/Photo Researchers. 56: (top) Stephen J. Krasemann/DRK Photo; (bottom) Stephen J. Krasemann/DRK Photo. 57: Stephen J. Krasemann/DRK Photo. 58-59: Russ Kinne/National Audubon Society Collection/Photo Researchers. 60: W. Perry Conway/Grant Heilman Photography. 60-61: Norman Myers/Bruce Coleman, Inc. 61: Annie Griffiths. 62-63: © Kathy B. Dawson 1978.

HIDE AND SEEK

Page 64: Jehangir Gazdar/Woodfin Camp, Inc. 66: (bottom left) Robert B. Evans; (top) Leonard Lee Rue III; (bottom right) Tom McHugh. 67: Paul E. Meyers. 68-69: James H. Carmichael, Jr. 69: Harvey Hansen. 70: (top left) Allan Power/Bruce Coleman, Inc.; (bottom left) Dr. F. G. Irwin; (top right) Larry West. 71: Douglas Faulkner/Sally Faulkner Collection.

SNUGGLING AND NUZZLING

Page 72: Kojo Tanaka/Animals Animals. 74: Robert P. Carr. 74-75: Michael C. T. Smith. 75: (top) Martin W. Grosnick; (bottom) Grant Heilman. 76: (top) Fred Bruemmer; (bottom left) Stephen J.

Krasemann/DRK Photo. 76-77: M. Austerman/Animals Animals.

LICK, SPLASH, AND SCRATCH

Page 78: Karl Maslowski. 80: (top) Robert Pollock; (bottom) Marilyn Krog. 81: Erwin and Peggy Bauer. 82-83: Lowell J. Georgia/National Audubon Society Collection/Photo Researchers. 83: Stephen J. Krasemann/DRK Photo.

LEARNING TO SURVIVE

Page 84: Charles G. Summers, Jr. 86: (top) Stouffer Enterprises Inc./Animals Animals; (bottom left) Stephen J. Krasemann/DRK Photo. 87: John Dommers. 88-89: (bottom) Dr. E. R. Degginger; (top) Norman Myers/Bruce Coleman, Inc. 90-91: (top) Javier Andrada; (bottom) Stephen Maslowski. 91: Roy Pinney. 92: (left) Phil A. Dotson/DPI (top right) Dr. E. R. Degginger; (bottom right) John MacGregor. 93: Kjell B. Sandved.

Library of Congress Cataloging in Publication Data

Main entry under title:

Ranger Rick's wonder book.

  Includes index.
  Summary: Describes how various baby animals are nurtured after birth, when they gain independence, why play is important in their development, and other aspects of their daily lives.
    1. Animals, Infancy of—Juvenile literature. [1. Animals—Infancy] I. National Wildlife Federation. II. Title: Wonder book.

QL763.R36 1982   591.3'9   82-60673
ISBN 0-912186-44-5

Acknowledgments

For their generous assistance, thanks are due naturalists Craig Tufts and Wendy Walker of the National Wildlife Federation's Education Center, and Douglas Miller, Director of the Federation's Institute for Wildlife Research. The staff of *Ranger Rick's Nature Magazine* was equally helpful in sharing information on the lives of young animals.

We would also like to recognize the ideas and suggestions of a new member of the Ranger Rick family, artist Alton Langford, whose Ranger Rick illustrations first appear in the pages of this book.

National Wildlife Federation

1412 16th Street, N.W.
Washington, D.C. 20036

Dr. Jay D. Hair
Executive Vice President

James D. Davis
Senior Vice President, Membership Development and Publications

Staff for this Book

Howard F. Robinson
Managing Editor

Victor H. Waldrop
Project Editor

Donna Miller
Design Director

Michael E. Loomis
Art Editor

Jeanne Turner
Designer

Alton Langford
Illustrator

Laura B. Ackerman
Research Editor

Dr. Raymond E. Johnson
Wildlife Consultant

Vi Kirksey
Editorial Assistant

Margaret E. Wolf
Permissions Editor

Priscilla Sharpless
Production Manager

Carol Kaufman
Production Artist